S0-BED-960

by Ted Cullman
illustrated by Manuel King

SCHOOL PUBLISHERS

Copyright © by Harcourt, Inc.

Requests for permission to make copies of any part of the work should be addressed to School Permissions and Copyrights, Harcourt, Inc., 6277 Sea Harbor Drive, Orlando, Florida 32887-6777. Fax: 407-345-2418.

HARCOURT and the Harcourt Logo are trademarks of Harcourt, Inc., registered in the United States of America and/or other jurisdictions.

Printed in China

ISBN 10: 0-15-350976-7
ISBN 13: 978-0-15-350976-6

Ordering Options
ISBN 10: 0-15-350601-6 (Grade 4 On-Level Collection)
ISBN 13: 978-0-15-350601-7 (Grade 4 On-Level Collection)
ISBN 10: 0-15-357929-0 (package of 5)
ISBN 13: 978-0-15-357929-5 (package of 5)

4 5 6 7 8 9 10 0940 12 11 10 09

Characters

Narrator	Makayla	Tracy	Steve
Mike	Karen	Carl	

Setting: The Green Mountains of Vermont

Narrator: It's a chilly morning in the Green Mountains of Vermont. A van pulls up outside a lodge, and a group of fourth-graders rush out the doors. They stand in awe as they take in the wondrous sights of the mountains— sparkling blue sky above them and miles of untouched, pristine forest below them.

Tracy: Look how high we are! There are little tiny towns down there somewhere.

Carl: Smell the air! It's like someone scrubbed the sky.

Makayla: Everything's so crisp and clean—and green! I like it here already.

Steve: I'm Steve, and this is Karen— welcome to Camp Adventure! Under our guidance, you're going to learn how to climb rocks—

Karen: –and get back down! You'll also learn how to find your way in the forest, and you'll get to know something about the plants and animals that live there. By the time we're done, you'll be seasoned and intrepid mountaineers!

Carl: I'm ready! Let's go climb a mountain!

Narrator: Later that morning, the group meets inside a building, where there is a wall that resembles a giant rock. They wear harnesses, helmets, and kneepads.

Carl: This isn't a mountain.

Makayla: Obviously—but it's tall enough for me!

Steve: There's a lot to learn about rock climbing, so we thought we'd practice indoors first.

Narrator: The kids watch as Steve and Karen show them how to find footholds in the rock wall. Then they take their turns.

Karen: You're doing great, Tracy! Just put your foot securely into the space, and hoist yourself up! Don't worry, the rope and harness are holding you.

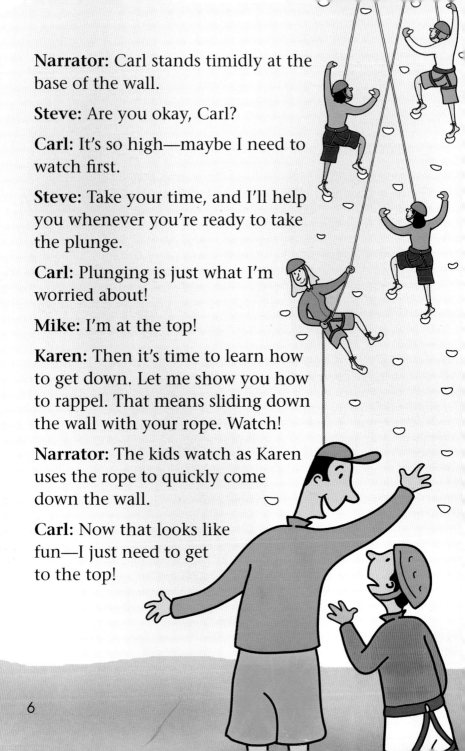

Narrator: Carl stands timidly at the base of the wall.

Steve: Are you okay, Carl?

Carl: It's so high—maybe I need to watch first.

Steve: Take your time, and I'll help you whenever you're ready to take the plunge.

Carl: Plunging is just what I'm worried about!

Mike: I'm at the top!

Karen: Then it's time to learn how to get down. Let me show you how to rappel. That means sliding down the wall with your rope. Watch!

Narrator: The kids watch as Karen uses the rope to quickly come down the wall.

Carl: Now that looks like fun—I just need to get to the top!

Narrator: After plenty of climbing practice, it's time to get out into nature. The kids follow Steve and Karen through a leafy green forest.

Carl: Hey—look at these peculiar tracks! I'll bet they belong to a mountain predator, like a cougar!

Steve: Actually, those are rabbit tracks.

Carl: I bet it was a scary rabbit, though.

Karen: Let's look at some of these plants and see which are edible and which we should stay away from.

Carl: I'm not eating plants!

Tracy: You would if you were hungry enough.

Carl: What are these plants?

Steve: That's poison ivy!

Narrator: The kids run from the poison ivy.

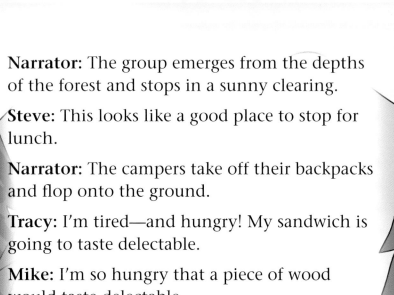

Narrator: The group emerges from the depths of the forest and stops in a sunny clearing.

Steve: This looks like a good place to stop for lunch.

Narrator: The campers take off their backpacks and flop onto the ground.

Tracy: I'm tired—and hungry! My sandwich is going to taste delectable.

Mike: I'm so hungry that a piece of wood would taste delectable.

Narrator: As the kids eat their lunches, Karen walks to the center of the circle and plants a stick into the ground.

Mike: What are you doing?

Karen: I'm going to find out where west, east, north, and south are.

Carl: My cell phone can show us our location with latitude and longitude. It also has maps.

Karen: That won't help if you don't know which direction is which, though. Also, what if your cell phone's battery runs out?

Makayla: Then you'd be in trouble!

Karen: Not really because we are going to use the sun to tell directions. See where the shadow of the stick ends? Let's put a pebble there to mark that point. Now let's wait a little while.

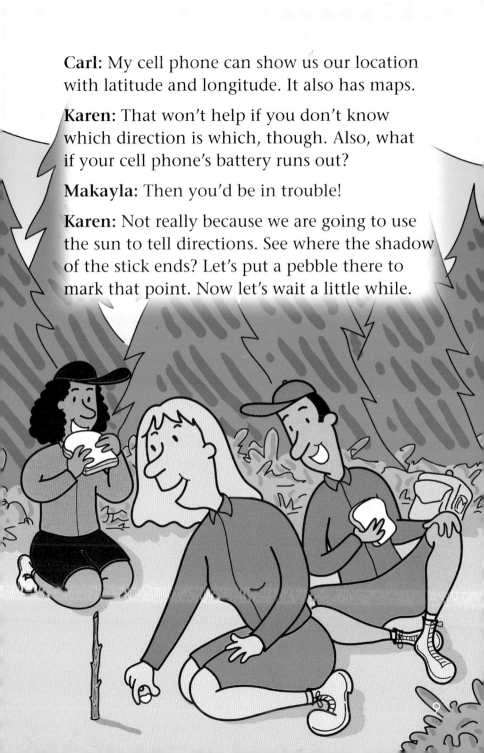

Narrator: Fifteen minutes pass, and then the group checks the stick again.

Tracy: The shadow moved!

Narrator: Karen puts a pebble where the shadow's new tip ends. Then she draws a line in the dirt between the two pebbles.

Karen: The shadow moved because the sun moved. The shadow moved toward the east. Now we know which way is east. We also know north is ahead of us and south is behind us. Now we can follow any set of directions we have!

Mike: We better not get lost at night, though.

Karen: Well, then we would have the stars.

Narrator: That night, the campers sit under a clear, star-filled sky. The fire, nearly out, slowly smolders in front of them.

Karen: See that bright star? That's *Polaris*, the North Star. If you keep that constantly ahead of you, then you'll always be traveling north.

Makayla: If you know where north is, then you also know south, east, and west.

Karen: Exactly.

Mike: I can't wait until tomorrow—I'm looking forward to climbing a real rock outside.

Steve: Practicing indoors undoubtedly can feel like drudgery. However, I guarantee that you're prepared to climb the rock tomorrow.

Narrator: The next morning dawns cool and crisp. The campers stand below an imposing, tall, gray slab of rock. They are already wearing their harnesses and helmets. Steve is at the bottom with them, while Karen is at the top of the rock, securing the ropes.

Tracy: It looks about the same size as the wall indoors. I'm ready to go!

Mike: I hope there are enough footholds.

Steve: There are plenty of footholds for you to find. You just need to take your time—it's not a race.

Makayla: Tracy and I can race if we want, though, can't we?

Tracy: First one to the top wins!

Narrator: Tracy, Makayla, and Mike begin to climb the wall. Carl hesitates at the bottom again.

Steve: Do you want to try, Carl? You did fine on the indoor wall once you got started.

Carl: I know, but the rock out here seems so big, and the ropes look so small and fragile.

Steve: They're not, though. You've seen me climb the wall with that rope, and I'm twice as big as you!

Carl: I guess . . .

Narrator: Tracy reaches the top and quickly rappels down the side of the wall.

Tracy: That was fun! I'm ready to go again!

Carl: Coming down is the fun part, so I guess I have to go up. Let's go!

Narrator: A few days later, the campers trudge out of the lodge to the van that waits to take them home.

Makayla: I can't believe camp is over. I'm really going to miss it.

Karen: We'll miss you, too. It's been a privilege to have you here.

Tracy: I never thought I'd love the mountains so much. I'll cherish every minute I had here.

Carl: I just wish I had time for one last climb.

Steve: Really?

Carl: Absolutely—I was slow to get started, but now I feel like I'm king of the mountain—or rock wall! I can't wait to come back next year!

Think Critically

1. If you could ask Karen a question, what would it be?

2. What effect does Tracy rappelling down the wall have on Carl?

3. What does the weather have to be like for the "shadow stick" to show which direction is which?

4. What words would you use to describe these campers?

5. Which part of the camp would you like best? Why?

Science

Gravity Facts Rock climbing can be difficult because of gravity. Look in your science book or on the Internet to find out more about gravity. Then write a short paragraph reporting your findings.

 School-Home Connection Explain to a family member what you learned from this story about using the sun and stars to find your way.

Word Count: 1,225